T0287423

CREWE IN THE DAYS OF BR BLUE

Michael Hitchen

AMBERLEY

First published 2019

Amberley Publishing
The Hill, Stroud
Gloucestershire, GL5 4EP

www.amberley-books.com

Copyright © Michael Hitchen, 2019

The right of Michael Hitchen to be identified
as the Author of this work has been asserted
in accordance with the Copyright, Designs and
Patents Act 1988.

ISBN 978 1 4456 9275 3 (print)
ISBN 978 1 4456 9276 0 (ebook)

All rights reserved. No part of this book may be
reprinted or reproduced or utilised in any form
or by any electronic, mechanical or other means,
now known or hereafter invented, including
photocopying and recording, or in any information
storage or retrieval system, without the permission
in writing from the Publishers.

British Library Cataloguing in Publication Data.
A catalogue record for this book is available from
the British Library.

Origination by Amberley Publishing.
Printed in the UK.

Introduction

Crewe as a railway centre needs little introduction, its history has been written many times before and its status as one of the country's most famous railway towns is in no doubt. Although the British Rail network had a number of other interesting railway locations, Crewe was unsurpassed: six routes meeting in the station, including the WCML, or 'Premier Line', as the LNWR proclaimed itself, a large marshalling yard, several motive power depots, carriage sheds, a number of separate smaller yards, wagon repair shops, rail-served PW depots and, of course, a locomotive works once the largest in the world. Needless to say there was lots for the enthusiast to see.

In the 1970s and early '80s railway operations and infrastructure remained that in many ways was similar to the steam age, which had not long since passed. Crewe as a railway junction retained much of its steam-era track layout, and though some change had taken place in the depots and workshops, a huge amount of interest remained. This was what is called the 'BR Blue' era, when the corporate image introduced in the mid-1960s was fully in place and blue locos and blue-grey coaches were the order of the day. Loco-hauled trains formed the majority of workings, with DMUs and EMUs only used for stopping service to local destinations such as Chester, Liverpool Lime Street, Altrincham and Shrewsbury, and the only longer workings to Lincoln and the North Wales coast. A major location on the WCML, AC electrics dominated Inter-City haulage. On any one day in the 1970s it would be possible to see all the different classes, with Classes 86 and 87 handling top link workings and the 81–85 on secondary, freight or parcels diagrams. The only regular diesel-hauled passenger diagrams were to Holyhead/Llandudno or Cardiff. These destinations were extended in the 1980s to west Wales and Liverpool or Manchester. The Euston–Holyhead – usually using Platform 2 on the Down, and 4 on the Up direction – exchanged traction at Crewe. This was generally a Class 40 in the early 1970s or later a Class 47, and was a fascinating everyday operation to observe.

Readers familiar with the extent of the local railway estate will know it was not possible to view everything from a single vantage point. Any location would have some compromise. Besides the obvious station platform end locations, usually at the south end to watch depot movements, the station car park could give north end activity and some limited visibly of the 'independents' – the freight-only lines that bypassed the station to the west and at a lower level, disappearing into tunnels under North Junction. To see WCML Inter-City trains at speed, I spent many an hour at Basford Hall Junction, viewing from the two nearby bridges or on the ground of the former sand siding location, to the south of Casey Lane. On the Shrewsbury (or Salop as many railwaymen called it) line, points of interest included the access walkway to the diesel depot from Gresty Road (Mornflake) Bridge. Occasionally you could get away with sitting on the path, watching freights on the steep climb up from Salop Goods Junction, and regular light engine and shunting trips made from Basford onto the Shrewsbury line.

Traction change for freight diagrams was common in this era and would take place either near Gresty Lane No. 1 signal box or in Basford Hall Yard. Further along the line, sidings used by the CCE department could be seen from the approach road that was accessed under the so-called 'Mucky Bridge' and often the Class 08, which worked the Pre-Assembly Depot (PAD), would stable nearby. On the opposite side of the line was Gresty Green Engineers Sidings, where the engine usually used to shunt was often a Class 25 or one of the last remaining Class 24s. Freight on this route was of interest, traditional wagonload workings (Carlisle to Severn Tunnel Junction), block company UKF trains, daily ballast workings from Bayston Hill, near Shrewsbury, and test trains from Crewe Work, which ran to Church Stretton. This was made up of Mk 1 coaches still in maroon livery. From 1976 the test trains also included brand new, often still in green undercoat, Class 43 power cars. They worked in a formation with the power car leading and a departmental coach and a Class 25 trailing. These only ran to Shrewsbury, where they turned on the triangle at the south end of the station so they could return with the power car leading again. Apart from the ubiquitous 25s, 40s and 47s, this line would occasionally see 'peaks' on summer Saturday-only holiday trains and some freights, Class 31s and 37s on Cardiff passenger trains, and earlier, the Western Region Diesel Hydraulics, but these would be a very rare sight. Passenger service had been Western Region Class 120, or briefly Class 123 DMUs, running as Class 2 trains. The upgrading of Cardiff passenger service to Class 1, saw Class 25s and Mk 1 stock. With the abolition of steam-heat stock, the route saw the unlikely introduction of Class 33s. The mainstay of Stoke line was the Class 120 Cross Country, or Class 104 (Birmingham RCW) DMUs on Derby/Lincoln trains. This line could see the rare appearance, at the time, of a Class 31 on the afternoon Peterborough Parcels. If a Class 20 or 44 was to make it to Crewe, it would be off the Stoke line.

By contrast, the WCML line to Liverpool, Stafford and branch to Manchester, were a solid diet of AC electrics, broken only by a few diesel-hauled freights, such as the BOC tanker trains to Ditton, or CCE departmental diagrams. Both the Liverpool and Manchester lines were served by the Class 304 EMUs on stopping trains. These would later be supplemented by Class 303 EMUs transferred from the Scottish Region, which caused some surprise when they appeared so far south. Finally the Chester line was made up of local DMUs to Chester and North Wales, loco-hauled trains (some starting in Crewe) to Holyhead or Llandudno, daily Freightliners to Holyhead, Stanlow Oil trains, and excursion traffic to the North Wales coastal resorts.

The town has been home to several locomotive depots over the years; the steam sheds of Crewe North (5A) and South (5B) were some of the largest in the region. By the 1970s it was still home to two large traction depots, stabling points and a carriage shed (coded CP), though there was no local DMU allocation at this time. Only the huge depots at Toton and Tinsley had larger allocations than the diesel depot, coded CD. The other depot for AC electric locos and Class 304 EMUs was coded CE – it was much harder to see as it was almost completely hidden from public view. Locos were stabled in the old north shed area until 1970, when the holding sidings between South Junction and the diesel depot became available. These were formerly parcels sidings. With the closure of the south shed, its ground was used to create new sidings for parcels stock, therefore releasing sidings to stable both diesel and electric locos. Alongside the north end of Platform 1, just below Nantwich Road, three sidings were used as electric-loco holding sidings. Additionally, locos were stabled in Basford Yard. The town had a number of shunter duties, including Crewe Works (two or three Class 08s), South Yard Parcels (2), Gresty Green PAD and Wagon Repair Shops (1), Up Parcel Sidings (1) and Basford Yard (2). A shunter could also be used on any trip duties, such as Stationery Store or Works, as required. If you were lucky enough to visit the depot, it was an unforgettable experience. Locos so familiar from the platform appeared quite different close-up from track level.

Crewe Locomotive Works, simply known locally as the 'Works', was legendary in enthusiast circles. Once the largest in the world, it had reduced from its original site in the V of the Liverpool and Chester lines, to sites west of Chester Bridge. Much of the original Works site lay derelict, and could be glimpsed off the top deck of a Crosville bus, especially the abandoned Deviation Works, where once the Chester main line had passed through the Works until it was re-routed to the south on its present alignment. It is unfortunate that this area, still rail connected, was not considered for a National Rail Museum at the time. The Works site that remained was still a huge site, often containing eighty to ninety locos undergoing all levels of repair or new build work. The annual open day was eagerly anticipated. It was possible to join a tour on a Sunday afternoon for a 20p donation to charity. These were meant for pre-organised groups, but the retired gent who guided them lived in our village, so we often used to tag along. Each week would see a new arrival, but in hindsight most locos were the same; though it was interesting to see how new loco builds progressed each week.

The station remained much the same as it was in the steam era. The station entrance in Nantwich Road had been rebuilt at the time of the WCML electrification in the early 1960s, but much at platform level, including the extensive platform canopies, remained unaltered. The station was one of constant activity: bays for local traffic at both ends, continuous arrivals and departures of Inter-City trains, with much else of interest for the rail enthusiast. The Euston–Holyhead trains would exchange traction and could be watched close up. Parcels and mail, from the prompt loading of calling trains where postal staff would load and unload in the brief minutes that a train was booked to call, would grow to mountains of brown sacks piled up around the station in the Christmas period – almost unimaginable in today's culture. Added to this was the more sedate making up of full parcel trains, which mainly used the old 1b and 2b bays that were no longer required for passenger traffic. Other bays were also used, especially at night or in the festive season. Unless you had some inside information it was not easy to find out about special workings, meaning an unusual working could appear at any time. This was part of the joy at the time, as you would not know what you may see. In today's age of information this is hard to imagine. Amongst these other workings were Motorail trains, excursion traffic (including stock from other regions) or even Pullmans that were (occasionally) charted for football specials. Just as occasional were the intriguing bullion workings, which appeared at a glance like a very short Freightliner but with one modified coach. At night the station became a different place. This was the time to see the Travelling Post Office (TPO) operations and long-distance sleeper trains. Being at the mid-point of the WCML, this type of coaching stock was not possible to see during usual daytime visits.

At the time it was not apparent, but this was the golden age of British Rail. It was one organisation joined together and, as we now know, the second most efficient in all of Europe. Sadly government interference and dogma has all but destroyed one of the best rail systems in the world. Capabilities and economies of the state-owned system are now impossible or ridiculously expensive. One only needs to look at what was achieved in rolling stock design and development, cascading of stock, highly skilled employment and in-house capabilities such as electrification. The movement towards railway privatisation was naive and could not replace the effectiveness of running one organisation – all staff being employed by the same board, working together for the benefit of the passenger. Possibly one day we will see the return of state-owned transport systems, re-investing profit for the user, in a progressive society.

Through this book I hope to take the reader back to a time when variety in livery may have been in short supply, unlike operational interest, which was far from limited. Only when we look back do we realise how much has changed. At the time it seemed, naively, that the railway would continue the same forever; now we know it was twilight of the state-owned railway. Thanks go to Ian Warmsley and Mike Mather for making some rare views available, to David Ingham for signal box photographs and extensive details, and to John Simcoe for sharing his S&T knowledge.

I would like to dedicate this book to my late uncle, Terry Higgins, a well-respected Crewe engine driver and a true railwayman. The second of four generations of drivers, working his way up from cleaner to fireman, then secondman, and, after many years, to certified driver. He retained his ticket to drive steam on the mainline right to the end of his career. We must remember this had been a tough job – difficult hours in all weathers – and even more so in the steam era when a fireman's duty, especially on the Crewe's Scottish Links, would have been hard manual work; the diesel era must have come as a culture change. Always happy to share his extensive knowledge, he was also an active enthusiast of the railways and other transport interests.

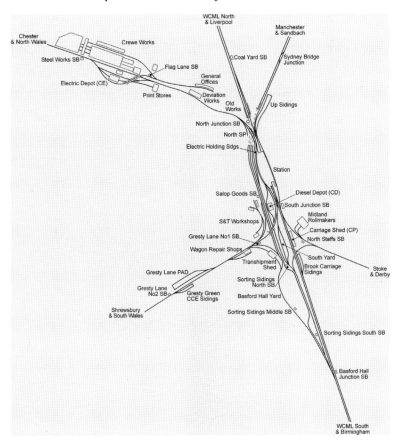

86039/87032, Basford Hall Junction

86039 and 87032 working in multiple to haul a southbound Freightliner out of Basford Yard onto the West Coast mainline Up slow in the early 1980s. Double-headed Freightliners more often ran overnight, which allowed the use of locomotive, usually allocated to passenger services, like the Class 87 seen here. A number of Class 86/0s were fitted with multiple equipment in the late 1970s to allow a working such as this one.

08694, Basford Hall Junction

The next three photographs were all taken during a fast line possession, just south of the A52 Newcastle Road Bridge. Starting with the unusual sight of a Class 08 out on the mainline, 08694 hauls a short engineers train on the Up fast line. Vacuum brake only, 08694 was allocated to Crewe Diesel Depot.

86254, Basford Hall Junction

With the engineer's trip shown above, just visible above the third coach, 86254 *William Webb Ellis* is relegated to the Down slow line – not an unusual event at weekends. Interestingly, the current is still on allowing electric traction.

25278 and 25164, Basford Hall Junction

25278 and 25164 pass on an engineer's train of recovered track panels. Another Class 25 is just visible under the A52 bridge in the background. 25278 and 25164 were allocated to Cricklewood and Crewe diesel, respectively, in the early 1980s.

40076, Casey Lane Bridge, late 1970s

A regular early evening working was a northbound BOC from the West Midlands to Ditton, just north of Runcorn. Usually hauled by a Class 40, here 40076 of Longsight depot slows its heavy train to enter Basford Yard and the independent lines.

25319 Approaching Basford Hall Junction, late 1970s

Usually a double-headed Class 25 duty, 25319 unusually has worked the Down fast from Stafford and crosses from the fast to slow line with the northbound 4F53 Forder's siding, Stewartby–Garston Fletliner (brick train) into Basford Yard in the early 1980s. This point work forms Crewe's southernmost crossovers, controlled by Basford Hall Junction Box. The ground behind the locomotives was once served by the 'Sand Sidings' but by this time the track had long since been lifted.

47147 Approaching Basford Hall Junction, late 1970s

Landore's 47147 hauls a Class 85 northbound on a Sunday drag whilst the wires were off for maintenance work. At this time weekend workings such as this were commonplace. Once Crewe was reached the 47 would be removed and the journey north would resume under electric power. Loco changing and coupling was a slick operation at Crewe Station – on such days Class 47s were lined up ready to take over services as required.

25209, Casey Lane Bridge, late 1970s

Accelerating away from Crewe but this time on the Up slow line, 25209 of Longsight (later Bescot) works an Air Braked Network from Ince and Stanlow, probably to Whitemoor yard in East Anglia. At this time, diesel workings south from Crewe over the WCML were limited to a few workings from the West Midlands and various CCE duties. These included long weld rail trains and ballast duties, but generally electric traction was used, even if it involved changing the locomotive further south.

82001, Casey Lane Bridge, late 1970s

Even in the late 1970s the majority of WCML freight services were block workings. Here, though, 82001 hauls a traditional mix of goods, including liquid chlorine tank wagons from Murgatroyd's works in Sandbach, spaced from the locomotive by two 24T coal wagons.

83001 and 85005, Casey Lane Bridge, late 1970s

Class 83/85 double head an oil train on the Up slow from Stanlow, near Ellesmere Port, to the Albion oil terminal, near Dudley. Apart from certain Freightliners, double-headed AC electric was unusual. The bridges at Basford and Casey Lane made good vantage points to watch WCML workings. Southbound express would be going at 'full chat' by this point, making number identification difficult.

86208, Basford Hall Junction

In the 1985 Crewe modernisation scheme, the majority of the station was out of use; some express services used the avoiding lines usually reserved for freights. Here a southbound express regains the WCML slow line, as 86208 *City of Chester* passes under Casey Lane Bridge as it accelerates out of the county of its name toward the Staffordshire border.

87024 *Lord of the Isles*, **Basford Hall Junction**

Moving slightly further north to Basford Hall Junction, 87024 will soon be applying its brakes for Crewe Station. Before modernisation few passenger trains ran non-stop through Crewe, and even if the train was not scheduled to stop, the mandatory speed restriction of 20 mph would need to be observed. Interestingly the first two coaches are Western Region Mk 2 stock.

Basford Hall Junction Box

Located between Basford Hall Bridge and Casey Bridge, Basford Hall Junction box was built by the LNWR in 1987. It originally housed eighty levers, later reducing to fifty-six. At this point the lines in the foreground contained the start of Basford Hall Yard. In the 1970s it was possible to sit on the wall at the ends of the bridge and watch freight working that used the yard and independent lines – something that would have been difficult to see in the station area. (David A. Ingham)

Sorting Sidings South Signal Box, 5 November 1990

The closed Crewe Sorting Sidings South signal box, located between the Down arrival line (in front of the signal box) and the Down slow independent line at the south end of Basford Hall yard. Sorting Sidings South was an unusual variant on the LNWR type 4 box in that instead of the usual 4-foot 6-inch-deep windows, its windows were 6 feet deep, a design more associated with the next LNWR box – the type 5. Opened *c.* 1901 it was fitted with a seventy-six-lever London & North Western Railway all-electric power frame as a result of major remodelling at Crewe. The signal box was extended by 15 feet 7½ inches at the step end around the start of the Second World War in order to accommodate a replacement seventy-five-lever Railway Executive Committee frame. The signal box closed on 22 October 1989 when the block section was extended to between Crewe Sorting Sidings North and Crewe Basford Hall Junction signal boxes. It remained derelict until demolition on 25 June 2000. (David A. Ingham)

24082 and 25148, Basford Hall Yard, 21 October 1976

24082 and 25148 stand in Basford Yard, near the Sorting Sidings Middle box, after working the 8K82 coal empties from Shotwick Sidings – a location that served the steelworks at Shotton, on the North Wales coast. Coal for these services generally came from the nearby North Staffordshire Coalfield.

Sorting Sidings Middle Signal Box, 5 November 1990

The closed Crewe Sorting Sidings Middle Up signal box, located between the Up arrival No. 2 (at the back of the signal box), and Up arrival No. 1 lines in Basford Hall Yard. The signal box was a British Railways London Midland Region type 15 design, which opened on 22 October 1961, and was fitted with a British Railways Gresty Road S&T individual function switch signalling panel. The box closed on 22 October 1989 when the running lines controlled by the signal box were converted to sidings. (David A. Ingham)

Sorting Sidings North Signal Box

Located between the Up through siding line and Up fast independent line at the north end of Basford Hall yard, Sorting Sidings North signal box is a British Railways type 15 design that opened in June 1962. It was originally fitted with a BR Gresty Road S&T individual function switch signalling panel. The box remains open today, with a replacement panel fitted in 2013. (David A. Ingham)

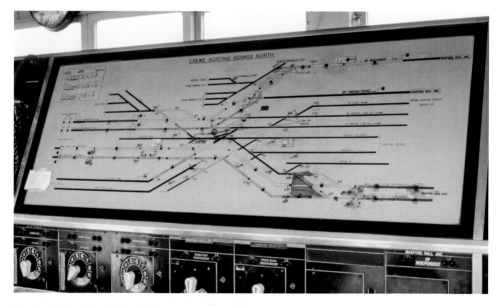

Sorting Sidings North Panel Diagram

The panel in Sorting Sidings North signal box illustrates the complexities of the independent lines. To the left are the lines to Gresty Lane No. 1, with and Down and Up independents that become the Liverpool, Manchester and Chester independents at Salop Goods Junction, the next box north. Note the engine shed sidings for the old Crewe South (5B) Engine Shed, which is still annotated. (David A. Ingham)

Sorting Sidings North Junction

This interesting view was taken standing on the fast independents, with the slow independents on the right and the curve up to Gresty Lane No. 1 on the left. After Salop Goods Junction, the lines become the Liverpool and Manchester independents. Such was the size of the railway estate in Crewe, locations such as this were only fleetingly visible from passenger trains and not possible to view from public access. (John Simcoe)

12082, South Yards, June 1970

With Sorting Sidings North box in the background, Class 11 shunter 12082 is seen stabled in the vicinity of the former Crewe South shed. It was withdrawn by BR in 1970 but found further work in the county with Shellstar at Ince Marshes (Ellesmere Port), remaining in use well into the 1980s. (Mike Mather)

47/87, Nantwich Station

An unidentified Class 47/4 hauls an 87, making for the unusual sight of a WCML drag heading through Nantwich Station towards Crewe. This line would only occasionally be used for such diversions, the train needing to run via Shrewsbury to Wolverhampton before electrification could be used again. The shorter route via Alsager must not have been available.

86321 and 47449, Nantwich Station

Another diversion working. 47449 hauls 86321 westbound through Nantwich Station, with the level crossing and signal box visible in the background.

33063 between Crewe and Willaston

Seen from Eastern Road in Rope, on the outskirts of Crewe, Hither Green allocated 33063 accelerates a Crewe–Cardiff working away from Crewe with the usual five-coach Cardiff train. As the diagram was allocated to Eastleigh-based type 3 locomotives, the use of Hither Green allocated 33s was a rarer sight.

47424 between Willaston and Crewe

ETH fitted Class 47/4, 47424, hauls a Saturday-only holiday working towards Rope Lane Bridge on the Shrewsbury line. There were three summer Saturday workings from the South West, which could also be hauled by a Class 45 or 46 'peak' – not a regular sight at Crewe at the time. On this occasion, though, a ubiquitous Class 47 was the motive power.

33211 between Crewe and Willaston, September 1986

Hither Green-based Hastings loading gauge 33211 hauls a Crewe–Cardiff working under Rope Lane Bridge, on the Shrewsbury line. The appearance of a 33/2 or 33/1 was unusual on these services. Class 33s had been introduced onto this diagram in June 1981, lasting until 1986.

47/87 between Crewe and Willaston

47504 hauls a Class 87 with another drag, leaving Crewe under Rope Lane Bridge. The only scheduled passenger services on this line, apart from the summer only West Country holiday workings, were the loco-hauled Crewe/Cardiff and DMUs on Crewe/Shrewsbury (later some to Swansea).

33007, Rope Lane Bridge, Wistaston/Rope

Photographed from Rope Lane Bridge and just leaving the extremity of the overhead electrification, 33007 accelerates away from Crewe with a Cardiff working. Just visible on the front of the bogie is the loco number, a practice common on Class 33s at the time. As usual the brake is marshalled in the centre of the train.

Shrewsbury Line, Gresty Lane

A mid-1960s view of a Brush type 4 approaching Crewe on the Shrewsbury line. Gresty No. 2 box is visible by the locomotive and just beyond the sidings at Gresty Green. On the right is the former Government Buffer Depot. The overhead electrification that extended on the Up main, as far as Rope Lane Bridge, was installed in the steam era to allow maximum flexibility of traction changing, but it was rarely used to these extremities. Most workings changed traction nearer to Gresty Lane No. 1 signal box. Note the lack of lineside vegetation!

Gresty Lane No. 2 Signal Box

LMS built to a classic LNWR design. Gresty Lane No. 2 box was opened by the LMS in 1928 with a nineteen-lever frame. It controlled the end of the loops at Gresty Green and the section west towards Willaston box. This box closed in October 1984, prior to the 1985 modernisation project.

25192, Gresty Green PW Sidings

With the pre-assembly depot (PAD) visible in the background, 25192 performs shunting duties in the Gresty Green PW Sidings. Unlike the PAD, which used a Class 08 shunter, these sidings south of the Shrewsbury line were shunted by a mainline locomotive as part of a trip duty. The sole surviving 24081 could often be found on this duty prior to withdrawal.

47289, Gresty Lane PAD Sidings

In the 1970s/early 1980s Freightliners were an unusual sight on the Shrewsbury line. Probably a diversion, 47289 of Thornaby crosses the 'Mucky Bridge' as it leaves Crewe. The lines in the foreground access the PAD that was built on the site of the Western Region Sidings.

Gresty Lane Wagon Repair Workshops

Looking towards Gresty Lane No. 1 box and Crewe Station. To the right is the former wagon repair workshop, then in use for the maintenance of CCE plant and machinery equipment. The site remains in use today as the DRS Depot. (John Simcoe)

Gresty Lane Junction No. 1 Signal Box

Gresty Lane signal box, located by the Up main line by Gresty Road underbridge, in Crewe. Gresty Lane signal box was a London & North Western Railway type 4 design that opened on 19 December 1898, and was fitted with a fifty-seven-lever London & North Western Railway Crewe all-electric power frame. The signal box was renamed Gresty Lane No. 1 after the opening of Gresty Lane No. 2 signal box, 1,449 yards to the east. This was possibly in 1913 when the lever frame was extended to sixty-six levers. The lever frame was replaced by a British Railways Chief Signals & Telecommunications Engineer's Works Crewe individual function switch signalling panel in late December 1978. Gresty Lane No. 2 signal box closed on 28 October 1984 and Gresty Lane No. 1 signal box was renamed Gresty Lane. The signal box was closed in December 2015, being replaced by Gresty Lane SCC – a signalling panel located in the existing Crewe SCC building, commissioned on 7 December 2015. The signal box was demolished on 8 May 2016. (David A. Ingham)

Gresty Lane Junction No. 1 Panel Diagram

Gresty Lane Junction No. 1 panel diagram shows the connections to Basford Hall Yard and Salop Goods Junction on the independent lines. When this photo was taken Gresty Lane No. 2 had closed, so the panel was amended simply to Gresty Lane. (David A. Ingham)

33008, Gresty Lane Junction, early 1981

Taken from the steps of Gresty Lane No. 1 box, 33008 has just crossed over the independent lines and is about to cross Gresty Lane Junction, which curves down to Salop Goods Junction on the left. The large building in the background was Midland Rollmakers, which once had a rail connection to the North Staffordshire line and its own shunting locomotives. Note the stored Class 25 and 40 locos in the Y sidings.

Salop Goods Junction Signal Box

Salop Goods Junction signal box is located by the Down Salop line on the Crewe avoiding lines, and is a London & North Western Railway type 4 design that opened in March 1901. It was fitted with a fifty-seven-lever London & North Western Railway Crewe all-electric power frame, in connection with major remodelling at Crewe. The signal box was extended to allow the power frame to be replaced by a sixty-five-lever Railway Executive Committee frame in 1938. (David A. Ingham)

Alsager East Signal Box, 25 May 1985

This box once controlled line to Sandbach and Audley, but at this time it controlled Up and Down loops and access to a spoil tip north of the line. It was located by the Up main line, a short distance west of the bridge over Linley Lane, near the site of former Alsager MPD. It's a North Staffordshire Railway type 1 design, fitted with a forty-five-lever McKenzie & Holland 1873 patent No. 5 frame. Signalling contractor McKenzie & Holland opened in 1880. This replaced an earlier signal box located a short distance to the west. The signal box controlled the junction with the Audley branch line until that line was closed on 7 January 1963, although the track remained for some years. The signal box closed on 2 June 1985 (officially closed on 21 July 1985) as part of the Crewe remodelling scheme. Signalling at Alsager passed to Crewe signal box, which was commissioned on 19 July 1985. The signal box carries a London Midland & Scottish Railway post-1935 design. (David A. Ingham)

Alsager Signal Box, 25 May 1985

Alsager Station signal box located by the Down main line, alongside Audley Road level crossing. A McKenzie & Holland type 1 design fitted with a McKenzie & Holland 1873 patent lever frame that opened *c.* 1872. The signal box was renamed from Alsager Station Junction. By the end of the decade it had a replacement twenty-two-lever McKenzie & Holland 1886 patent No. 11 and a gate wheel, which was installed in 1890. In the first few years of the twentieth century it was reduced in height by 9 feet. The gate wheel was removed when the level crossing gates were replaced by manned barriers on 15 December 1974. The signal box closed on 3 June 1985 as part of the Crewe remodelling scheme, with signalling at Alsager passing to Crewe signal box, which was commissioned on 19 July 1985. (David A. Ingham)

Radway Green Signal Box, 25 May 1985

Alongside Radway Green Road level crossing, Radway Green signal box was the location of a Royal Ordnance factory, which had its own station served by non-advertised staff trains. The factory had a railway connection and had its own MOD shunting locomotives. It had a North Staffordshire Railway type 1 design fitted with a McKenzie & Holland lever frame, built *c.* 1881 and replacing an earlier signal box. The lever frame was a gate wheel (1) and twenty levers (2-21), which was replaced by a twenty-lever frame installed by British Railways. The level crossing gates were replaced by manned barriers on 29 May 1977. The signal box closed on 3 June 1985 as part of the Crewe remodelling scheme, with signalling at Radway Green passing to Crewe signal box, which was commissioned on 19 July 1985. The next box towards Crewe, on the North Stafford line, was North Stafford Sidings, only 550 yards away from Crewe South Junction. It was closed on 21 October 1973. (David A. Ingham)

Crewe Diesel Depot Holding Sidings

The Shrewsbury lines leading away from the junction in the foreground, seen from a passing train. A line of withdrawn Class 40s and 25s stand at the end of the holdings sidings.

Crewe South Junction Signal Box

Crewe South Junction signal box with its Westinghouse Brake & Signal Co. Ltd L-style power lever frame, was opened and commissioned on 29 September 1940 by the London Midland & Scottish Railway, as part of the re-signalling scheme for Crewe Station. It was built to a non-standard ARP design, with 15-inch-thick reinforced-concrete walls and reinforced-concrete roofs that were 18 inches thick. It was fitted with a 227-lever Westinghouse L frame and worked in conjunction with Crewe North Junction, with its 214 levers, to control the Crewe area. The box was reduced to a non-block post on 2 June 1985 during the major renewals at Crewe Station. The signal box remained in use for forty-eight years until its operation was taken over by Crewe Signalling Centre on 6 June 1985. The building still stands in place today. (David A. Ingham)

86003, 86038, Electric Holding Sidings

86038 was in the 86/0 sub-class. It was restricted to 80 mph and was used mainly on freight working. Between the diesel depot and the running lines were a number of lines used to stable electric locos between duties, therefore avoiding the run to the less convenient location of the electric depot. Unusual in this view is the Class 56, buffered to 47228. New to the area, the Class 56s were being used on MGR workings from North Staffordshire Coal Field, though they continued to be allocated to Toton Depot.

86319, Electric Holding Sidings

Photographed on the same occasion as 86003/038, is 86319, one of nineteen Class 86/0 modified by the use of SAB resilient wheels, which improved running and allowed an increase in maximum speed to 100 mph.

86033, 08927, Crewe South Junction, 11 June 1978

08927 propels 86033 across Crewe South Junction in an unknown manoeuvre. The orange multiple working boxes had recently been fitted to 86033, mainly for heavy nighttime Freightliners, which required two AC electrics. This modification allowed multiple working with Class 87s, which were built with this capability.

24063, Crewe Diesel Depot, 3 October 1978

24063 stands with 25036 at the rear of the diesel depot. At this time Crewe was associated with Class 24, with the depot being the last in the country with this class on allocation.

08823, Crewe Diesel Depot, 12 January 1991

Crewe had an allocation of approximately twenty-two Class 08 diesel shunters. Apart from all the local duties, the depot also supplied shunters for Stoke and Shrewsbury. Nearby, Chester had its own allocation of Class 08s. Northwich retained a stabling point but, although relatively close, had its requirement for a couple of shunters out stationed from Allerton. 08823 is a dual-braked variant.

Crewe Diesel Depot, June 1970

Taken at the south end of the depot building, which was less visible to the public, Class 08, 50 and 40 stand outside awaiting attention. At the start of the 1970s the entire Class 50 fleet was allocated to Crewe for hauling trains on the yet to be electrified section to Glasgow. They were often used in pairs on these WCML passenger working, but could be found on many duties, including freight, throughout the North West. (Mike Mather)

D423, Crewe Diesel Depot, 1970

An interesting photo taken of Class 50 D423, standing on the road behind the depot. The independents are visible to the left, running at a lower level. At one time there was a direct connection from this line to the Chester independent, but this was removed in the late 1960s. (Mike Mather)

Class 40 D377, Crewe Diesel Depot, early 1970s

Both still in green livery, Class 47 1859 stands with Class 40 D377. The locos are standing on one of the depot's fuelling roads, with the canopy of Platform 1 visible in the background. D377 would be renumbered 40077 and would be withdrawn in 1983.

Crewe Diesel Depot, 26 May 1980

A view from the end of Platform 2 enjoyed by spotters for many years. This view includes the last remaining Class 24, 24081, with its white-painted buffer.

47539, Crewe Diesel Depot, August 1978

With its wheel rims picked out in white and in immaculate condition, locally allocated 47539 has been prepared for a special duty – possibly the Royal Train. In the background is the depot's snowplough, and just visible is a Sandite coach, converted from a DMU driving car and fitted with tanks and dispensing equipment. This was in order to apply the Sandite mixture to the railhead in areas where wheel slipping was an issue.

D843, Old Yard, 15 May 1968

A rare visit of a Western Region 'Warship'. D843 *Sharpshooter* pushes its stock from the 3K26 parcels working from Shrewsbury. The location is the Old Yard, which had been used for parcels stock until 1970, when the north depot stabling point and south depot had closed. These sidings were modified for stabling locomotives and, in turn, the site of the south shed (5B) was re-laid with new sidings for parcels stock.

Crewe Diesel Depot

A nighttime view from the end of Platform 1 shows a typical selection of locomotives stabled in the depot and the holdings sidings. Also visible are the snowplough and the CM&EE breakdown crane, one of two that were stabled at Crewe in the 1970s – the other, painted red, was a steam-powered version.

33209, Crewe South Junction, 2 July 1983

Though Class 33 became the usual motive power for Cardiff trains, the sight of either of the two sub-classes was a rare event, so 33209 would have caused some local excitement when it appeared on this duty.

08701, Crewe South Junction

The south end bays, 1b and 2b, were used exclusively for parcels from the 1970s, often requiring two Class 08s. Movements between the bays and the parcels sidings on the site of the old south shed were continuous. 08701 undertakes one of these movement, which at times involved propelling lengthy rakes. Around Christmas there would be so many parcels and mail bags on the platform it would not be possible to get to the platform ends.

86232, Crewe South Junction, 1 June 1985

86232 *Harold Macmillan* prepares to make its station stop on Platform 2. Visible is some of the preparatory work for the modernisation, which would see much of the station closed the following day for six weeks.

83001, Crewe South Junction, 22 February 1979

Drawing its long parcels train out of the south parcels sidings, 83001 uses the Down through line parallel to Platform 2, in February 1979. The mix of parcels stock, many dating from pre-nationalisation, can be seen in the train. The amount of parcels and mail cannot be understated in this period. With a Royal Mail sorting office connected to the station by its own subway, activity was constant throughout the day. At night TPO workings would be booked to connect in the station.

47413, Crewe South Junction

An early 1980s southbound departure – probably on a Sunday as diesel traction is in use. Note the two AC electrics in the slip siding. More at home on an east coast express working, Gateshead's 47413 hauls a rake of early Mk 2 stock, a formation usually used on Liverpool–Birmingham and certain inter-regional services at this time.

86252, Crewe South Junction, 13 May 1979

With its cast Inter-City symbol still in the centre, unnamed 86252 accelerates southwards in May 1979, past the electric Holding Sidings and diesel depot. This locomotive was named *The Liverpool Daily Post* in 1980.

25051 and 224, Crewe Station, 6 April 1983

Amongst April showers, enthusiasts watch a sand working from either Oakmoor or Culdron Low quarries in the Leek area, bound for the glassmaking industries around St Helens. These workings later gained barrier wagons to protect the loco crews from sand blowing onto them. The second locomotive, 25224, was one of a small batch of Crewe-allocated, boiler-fitted 25s for use on Crewe–Cardiff services.

31127, Crewe South Junction, 1986

An unusual Research Centre working, powered by 31127 with Test Car 2 and a European open wagon. Test Car 2 was ADB975397, a mobile laboratory used in slip and brake testing.

97201, Crewe Station, early 1980s

Former 24061 was allocated the number ADB968007 when transferred to departmental use in 1975. Renumbered 97201 in 1979, it was often used to power the RTC Tribometer train, which is seen working on the south through road alongside Platform 4. The first coach is Tribology Section ADB 975046, Laboratory 11. It was used to study the friction between the wheel and rail. Both this coach and the locomotive survive in preservation.

08907, South Parcel Bays, late 1970s

Dual-braked 08907 is seen standing in the parcel bay at the south end of Crewe Station alongside Platform 2. These two platforms were used solely for parcels. One or two Class 08s spent all day forming parcel stock between these platforms and the South Yard. Sadly this traffic has been lost to our overcrowded roads, which can only be viewed as a backwards step.

XDE87813, South Parcel Bays, 27 March 1981

When British Rail existed as one organisation, internal transfer working, such as between Crewe Station and Crewe Stationery Store, were possible. The Stationery Store were situated in Flag Lane alongside the Chester line, just before the electric depot. This former 'Blue Spot' fish van was a common sight at the south end, waiting to be tripped as required.

Platform 1, Crewe Station, 1980

Looking north along Platform 1 towards Crewe Station 'A' cabin. To the left, under the canopy, can be seen the horse landing dock siding, once used for Motorail traffic.

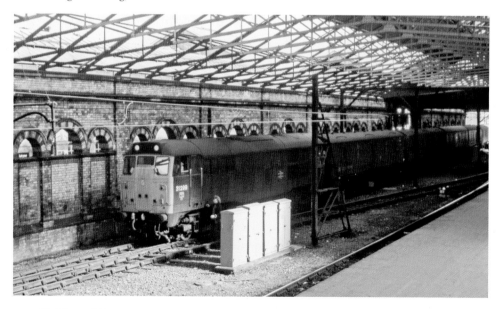

31299, Up Through Line, Crewe Station, 24 April 1979

Each weekday around 16.10 the Peterborough parcels would arrive at Crewe. This working would often produce a Class 31, a rare sight at Crewe in this era. Here, March-based 31299 stands on the Down through line, about to be uncoupled from its stock. Once light engine, it would run forward across North Junction using the Chester line to reverse and run back to the diesel depot.

08702, Former Up Through Line, Crewe Station, 30 October 1990

Long-term resident of Crewe Diesel Depot, dual-braked 08702 attaches a GUV (ex-newspaper corridor connection fitted) to an Up parcels working. By the time this view was taken this line was no longer in use as the non-stop Down line.

Platform 1, Crewe Station, 17 September 1982

A quiet moment on Platform 1 looking south towards the diesel depot, which can be seen in the gap of the valance.

Crewe Station A Signal Box

Crewe Station A signal box stood between Platform 1 and Down through line 1. Built by the LNWR in 1907, with a twenty-six-lever electric power frame, it was a non-standard variation on a type 5 design, as it had a flat roof. Closure came after the modernisation programme in July 1985. Previously there had been a similar B box opposite, between Platform 2 and the Down through. This box controlled access to the Holding Sidings and diesel depot.

Platform 2, Crewe Station, 2 March 1985

Looking north along Platform 2, with one of the two footbridges visible just beyond the clock. Prior to the summer 1985 modernisation programme this was the main northbound platform. The Down through line and wall of Platform 3 can be seen to the right.

85029, Platform 2, Crewe Station

85029 displays its 1Z14 head code, indicating a special working – probably a BR organised Merrymaker or Mystery Tour, which were popular throughout the 1970s.

25063, Platform 4b, late 1970s

25063 sets back onto the stock for a Cardiff working after being released by a Class 08 shunter. The bays at Crewe then lacked any crossovers to allow traditional run rounds to take place. Cardiff workings, being loco hauled, required a shunter to haul the stock clear. Enthusiasts could take advantage of this free trip to get a closer look at the loco at the depot.

Class 120 DMU, Crewe South Junction, 1 June 1985

Class 120 cross-country 53713/59258/52667 of Derby Etches Park depot, departs, unusually, from Platform 4b for Derby and Cleethorpes. These service normally departed from Platform 5b. This change was probably in connection with the Crewe modernisation works, which were about to take place. Chester-allocated Class 120 DMU used these bays for Shrewsbury local workings – note the original centre car is still in use. These were generally replaced by Metro-Cammell centre cars by the mid-1980s.

Class 120 DMU, Platform 4b, February 1973

Prior to 1977 Cardiff diagrams were allocated to Class 120 cross-country DMUs allocated to Cardiff depot, and often coupled to single-car DMU for additional traction. The timetable was upgraded, which saw the introduction of hauled services using Mk 1 coaches and Class 25s.

7053, Crewe Station, 12 March 1971

A very rare view of a Hymek at Crewe. Substituted instead of the more usual DMU Class 35, 7053 is seen drawing up to Platform 4b. Its coaching stock has been pulled away by a Class 08, allowing the loco to be released. The head code should be 2V67, though the usual diagrammed DMU head code was only two characters, so would display 'B5'. (Ian Warmsley)

33006, Crewe Station, 6 March 1984

33006 is seen standing in Platform 3, the only platform then regularly used for both north and south workings. Class 33s were introduced to Crewe–Cardiff working in June 1981, which also allowed ETH coaching stock to be used. These workings were later extended to Manchester and Bangor, then by 1986 to Llandudno Junction and Holyhead. Class 33 use came to an end in September 1986 when 37/4 became the norm. This working, probably a Cardiff working but using Platform 3, unusually includes a BG behind the engine.

33020, Platform 4b, August 1982

Eastleigh-allocated 33020 stands at the end of Platform 4b, after working the 116 miles from Cardiff Central. This was the usual platform for Cardiff workings. The change from locally allocated 25s to the Southern Region was an unusual development. Even though the class worked these services for several years they always remained an incongruous sight so far north. Platform 3b in the foreground was used for Shrewsbury line stopping service and, up to 1966, Market Drayton locals as well.

33033, Platform 4b, early 1980s

Eastleigh Class 33s were the usual locos allocated to the diagram that included Cardiff–Crewe workings. Again in Platform 4b, the engine is ready for its long trip through the picturesque Welsh Marches to the Welsh capital. Note the two AC electrics standing in the bank loop ready to take over southbound WCML trains from diesel haulage.

33002, Crewe Station, 6 December 1985

Photographed at 21.30, 33002 runs through the station on the Down fast through line, which had been installed in the 1985 station modernisation. Before 1981 the Southern Region-allocated locomotive rarely, if ever, ventured north of Birmingham, but by this time the sight of a Class 33 was a common sight in south Cheshire.

Crewe Station, 19 September 1982

It's hard to imagine today's Down fast was an electric loco stabling road with a buffer stop just beyond the 86/3 loco, seen stabled on this siding in this September 1982 photo. Also visible are some of the huge number of mail bags, inconceivable today, left on the platform awaiting loading – often into a brake van of a passenger service.

87101 *Stephenson*, **Platform 4, late 1970s**

Sporting its non-standard silver nameplate, 87101 was the unique thyristor power control 87/1 sub-class loco. It was named *Stephenson* in October 1977, the name being transferred from 87001. Although allocated to normal passenger service, it remained an unusual sight in general use, occasionally appearing on Research Centre special workings.

86206 *City of Stoke on Trent*, **1 June 1985**

86206 *City of Stoke on Trent* stands light engine at the south end of Platform 4, with the platform also being occupied by a Class 25. This was the start of the Crewe modernisation programme, which affected services in June and July 1985. Behind the loco work has yet to start on the Up and Down fast line, which now passes between these platforms. Catenary stanchions G15793 and 100 would be removed and the new OLE support is visible above and behind G157100.

86328, Crewe Station, 1 June 1985

86328 is seen on the last day of the old station layout – 1 June 1985. The next day the modernisation programme would see the station out of general use until 21 July. This was one of the last occasions both Platforms 4 and 5 would be occupied by southbound expresses. Once reopened, the erstwhile Platform 4 would become northbound Platform 6.

86220, Crewe Station, mid-1970s

Standing in the bank siding at the south end of Platform 4, un-named 86220 waits to take over a diesel hauled service from Holyhead. The coupling and uncoupling was a routine procedure for British Rail, allowing the correct traction to be used accordingly. Today's railway appears to have lost the ability to do simple railway tasks such as this.

83009 Departs Platform 3, early 1980s

With 86251 *The Birmingham Post* stabled in the background, 83009 departs from Platform 3 with a southbound, probably special, working. The use of the early electrics, especially 82/83/84, on passenger workings by the early 1980s was an unusual sight, though they could appear on specials and Motorail workings.

25221, Crewe South, 1978

Running light engine 25221 out of Platform 4, past the slip siding. 25221 had recently been transferred from Cricklewood to Crewe diesel in 1978. Boiler fitted, it was a regular on Cardiff working. Interestingly, it was also fitted with a telephone plug point, just visible between the lamp irons, for Royal Train duties to locations where the usual Class 40 or 47s were not permitted.

47331, Platform 3, mid-1970s

In the summer, non-heat 47/3 could be pressed into passenger service, such as 47331 of Toton depot, which was more accustomed to freight traffic in the East Midlands. Seen here drawing away from a Holyhead–Euston service in Platform 3 to allow electric traction to haul it south.

37408, Crewe Station, September 1985

The new order between South Wales and the North West was the Class 37/4. Here we see 37408 *Loch Rannoch* standing at the south end of Platform 6 (previously 4). This loco had been numbered 37289 in 1974 and throughout the 1970s was allocated to Cardiff Canton depot, appearing occasionally on Cardiff–Crewe duties. Rebuilt at Crewe Works to 37408 in 1985, it is seen in ex-works condition before going back to Glasgow Eastfield for use mainly on the West Highland line.

Crewe Station Derby Bays

Renumbered Platform 4, after its long identity as 5b, this south end bay was used for cross-country services to Derby and Lincoln. These services were monopolised by Class 120 DMUs, allocated to Derby Etches Park. Enthusiasts will remember that the DMU fleet had windows at the time that, if the blinds were left up, enabled passengers to enjoy the driver's view out of the front.

50030, Crewe Station, 7 December 1985

Once the transfer to the Western Region was completed in 1976, the sight of a Class 50 at Crewe became very rare, especially once works responsibility was transferred from Crewe to Doncaster in 1977. After this it would not be until late 1985 that a diagram would bring them back to the station. Here 50030 *Repulse* is seen ready to depart with the 02.09 mixed passenger and TPO working to Cardiff.

E3069, Crewe Station, 28 August 1973

Same location as the Class 50, Class 85 displays it pre-tops number E3069 whilst standing at Platform 5 on the 1V90 Manchester Piccadilly–Plymouth working. Whilst reporting numbers were displayed, workings could be identified by referring to working timetables or local knowledge. E3069 would be renumbered 85014 in 1973. The fleet of 85s were allocated to Crewe Electric Depot for much of their life.

85026, Crewe Station, 1984

Prior to the modernisation of the station, 85026 passes with an unidentified special working. Note the Class 33 standing on Platform 4b with a Cardiff train.

E3084, Crewe Station, February 1973

Class 85 E3084 is stabled in the siding between Platform 2 and No. 2 through line. In the 1970s electric locos could be found stabled around the station, according to traffic requirements. E3084 would be renumbered 85029 in 1973.

87026, Crewe Station, July 1981

87026 *Redgauntlet*, on a Scottish-bound express, drifts non-stop on the No. 2 Down through line alongside Platform 2. Between this line and the platform line can be seen the stabling siding, which ended just under the bridge. By this time it was rarely used.

434, Crewe Station, 7 April 1973

Having just replaced an AC electric, Class 50 No. 434 stands at the north end of Platform 2 with the 1S57 for Glasgow Central. Once electrification was extended, traction changeover was moved north to Preston until 1974, when full Anglo-Scottish electrics services were introduced. Note the parcels stock being unloaded on Platform 1.

1923, Crewe Station, 7 April 1973

Seen on the same day as 434, Class 47, 1923 (later 47246) waits departure from Platform 2 with a northbound special working. The multi-storey Rail House dominates the background.

86212, Crewe Station, 3 November 1981

An enthusiast admires 86212 *Preston Guild* as it awaits departure from Platform 1 in 1981. 86212 was named in 1979, though it was originally to be named *City of Edinburgh*. In the background a Class 47 works up the Chester independent line, probably with a Holyhead-bound Freightliner.

47452, Crewe Station, April 1977

Crewe-allocated ETH-fitted 47452 draws back onto a Holyhead train, and moments after the Class 86 haulage from Euston had been detached. Shunting staff made this a slick operation, though I remember a Class 87 being detached by accident, running forward partway across the North Junction before the error was realised, then promptly reversed back to be re-coupled to its train, all taken in their stride by the railwaymen on duty.

Crewe Station, February 1973

A scene that illustrates the traction changeover so typical of the early 1970s. A Class 86 stands in the background after working a service from the south, whilst a Class 50 runs into Platform 3 to take the train north to Glasgow. In the background are the original works buildings, in the V between the Chester and Liverpool lines, though out of use by this time.

86009, Crewe Station, 1984

86009 waits departure from Platform 2a with the 1P35, 15.13 Crewe–Barrow. Unusual as most electric loco hauled services did not start from Crewe. First stop would be Warrington, with a traction change at Preston or Carnforth for the un-electrified Cumbrian coast line to Barrow.

40016, Crewe North Junction, late 1970s

Though an everyday sight at Crewe, at the time the depot had no allocation of Class 40s – LMR locos being allocated to Longsight, Springs Branch or Carlisle. Kingmoor's 40016 had lost its name, *Campania,* by this time. In the late 1970s Class 40s were still used on regular passenger workings to North Wales, Holyhead and Llandudno, and excursions along the coast.

47371, Chester Independents, 1985

Tinsley's 47371 climbs up the Chester independents with a Northbound parcels working. Whilst the station was being remodelled numerous workings were diverted via the independent lines or, in the case of local services, replaced by feeder bus services. The line appears to be worked by hand signalling, with the approaching signal CE131 covered out of use.

83005, North Junction, October 1975

The early AC electric-type AL3 became Class 83 in the TOPS system. Fifteen were built during 1960 and 1962. The AL3s were fitted with problematic mercury-arc rectifiers, resulting in the class being stored at locations including Bury loco shed in the late 1960s. Additional traction requirements from the electrification from Weaver Junction to Glasgow prompted the rebuilding and reinstatement of the entire class.

85005, Crewe Station, mid-1970s

The use of Class 85 and 81 on secondary passenger services was common. Here 85005 departs from Platform 1 with a northbound service. The open land in the background was the site of the large north shed (5A) and, for a period, a stabling point.

Crewe North, February 1973

Again looking towards the former Crewe North (5A) site, a Class 83 stands in Platform 1 and a 25 awaits in the un-electrified diesel locomotive holding siding. Behind the gantry can be seen one of the last remaining tall chimneys that once dominated the Crewe skyline.

83007, Crewe North, October 1974

83007 departs across North Junction with a rake of Mk 1s – probably a secondary service, as early Mk 2s were in use by this time. As the 1970s progressed the use of the Class 82–84 on passenger working became increasingly rare.

86247, Crewe North, September 1974
Recently renumbered from E3192, 86247 clearly displays the flexicoil suspension that allowed 100 mph running, and was fitted from 1971.

D309, Crewe North, 1970
Class 40 D309 arrives into Platform 3 with a train from Holyhead. Just visible is a Class 47, stabled in the remains of Crewe North Depot. The approach roads were retained as a stabling point until 1970, when the diesel depot was enlarged to include the Holding Sidings, on the former Old Yard Parcel Sidings, between the South Junction and the diesel depot site.

Crewe North, February 1973

With snow on the ground, another traction exchange takes place as a Class 86 draws off its train. The former Crewe North stabling point was out of use by this date. A Class 304 stands in Platform 3a with a local service to Liverpool Lime Street.

47432 and 47205, Crewe North

Bescot's 47432 receives assistance from Crewe's 47205 with a Holyhead train in the early 1980s. Conditions like this could cause issues with point-work, evidence of which can be seen in the foreground. Hopefully one of the locos was able to supply carriage heating!

81012, Crewe North Junction

Looking across the North Junction towards Macon Way, 81012 works a Freightliner through the station. This was a slightly unusual occurrence as the majority of freight working from the Liverpool and Manchester lines would use the independent lines to bypass the North Junction and station area.

08701, Platform 4, 6 March 1976

Vacuum-only braked 08701 trundles through Platform 4 from the North Junction. At this time the station, besides the usual arrivals and departures, was full of other movements from light engines to parcel shunting. In 1976 there was a requirement for one Class 08 at the north end to shunt Up Parcel Sidings alongside the Manchester line.

50040 and 86256, Platform 4, mid-1970s

Timed to arrive at 16.24, 50040 hauls 86245 on the 1M35, the 11.00 Glasgow Central to Euston, arriving there at 18.51. This was a Sunday and the Class 50 had probably hauled the train from Preston or Warrington, to allow the overhead electrification to be turned off for maintenance. 50040 was one of the last Class 50s to leave Crewe for the Western Region, in 1976.

86223, Platform 4, 26 January 1980

86223 *Hector* prepares to stop in Platform 4 with a Euston express. When the hauled Mk 3 coaches were built only a limited number of buffet coaches were included and no brake facilities at all. Mk 1 BGs, seen here, and buffet cars were fitted with B4 and B5 bogies to allow 100 mph running.

87003, Crewe North Junction, 17 July 1975

Unnamed and only a couple of years old, 87003 use the Up through line as it runs non-stop with a Euston bound 'Royal Scot' service. 87003 was named *Patriot* in 1978, and would be exported to Bulgaria in 2008.

87027, Crewe North Junction, 24 July 1979

87027 *Wolf of Badenoch* comes off the Liverpool line and crosses to the Up through line, not calling at Crewe. In 1979 this type of train, with Mk 3 coaches and relatively new 5,000 horsepower Class 87 traction, represented top link WCML services. Note the two Class 08s: one in shunt neck off Platform 4, the other shunts the Up Parcel Sidings alongside the Manchester line.

86210, Platform 4, early 1980s

86210 *City of Edinburgh* prepares to make its station stop in Platform 4 with a southbound express. The red mail trolleys on the platform in the foreground were found all over the station, evidence of the huge amount of mail and parcels handled every day. They also found popularity with the enthusiast community.

Class 101, Platform 9, 10 August 1985

The recently completed modernisation works are visible as a three-car Class 101 departs for Chester from the renumbered Platform 9, in August 1985. Previously Platform 4a, it was used mainly by Manchester/Altrincham stopping services, but could also access the Liverpool line. The adjacent Platform 3a could be used for Liverpool, Manchester or Chester local services. This platform was realigned in the 1985 modernisation programme, after which it could only be used for Chester line workings.

Platform 9, 8 December 1985

Another Chester local, this time formed of Class 108s, M53625 and M54213, from Platform 9. A result of the 1985 modernisation programme was the removal of the old north-facing 1a and 2a bays – traditionally the departure lines for Chester and Liverpool local workings.

Class 101, Platform 9, 6 December 1985

Class 101s, M54344 and M51183, stand in Platform 9 after arrival from Chester on the evening of 6 December 1985. Certain DMU workings would extend along the North Wales line, but a number made the short no-station run to Chester only. Crewe at this time had no DMU allocation of its own, with all regular duties being covered by Chester or Derby.

86233, Northbound Through Line, 21 September 1985

86233 stands on the Down through line with the 01.35 Crawley to Manchester Mayfield, in September 1985. The 1985 modernisation programme introduced northbound Down through workings to what had been the Up side of the station, which was an unusual sight for anyone familiar with the station layout previously.

304011, Crewe North Junction, 1985

The new order, post-summer 1985, a Liverpool Lime Street stopping service to Crewe arrives into Platform 5 – the only platform to retain its number after July 1985. These workings could use the new renumbered Platform 1 (formerly 6) or the bay Platform 10. This unit possibly ran out of service to the carriage shed after arrival. The 304 is in its original four-car formation. The refurbishment and reduction to three cars was well underway at this time.

25042, Crewe, Platform 3, 22 September 1979

Crewe was always a popular location for enthusiasts, but the large amount on Platform 4 gives a clue to the occasion of a works open day. 22 September 1979 was such a day. Seen here is Crewe Diesel's 25042, a boiler-fitted variant for Crewe. Cardiff passenger services run light engine from the north end of Platform 3 in front of the large crowds.

310069, Crewe Up Through, 10 August 1985

Even though they could be seen close by at Stoke, on services to Manchester Piccadilly, Class 310 EMUs were never a common sight at Crewe; as in this case, only on special workings. Two units, led by 310069, pass non-stop on a 'Footex' from Manchester to Wembley for the FA Charity Shield (between Manchester United and Everton), on 10 August 1985.

86221, Crewe Station, 1985

86221 *Vesta* takes the Up through line with a southbound excursion or special working. Note the Crewe Signalling Centre under construction in the background.

87029, Platform 6, Crewe Station, 1984

Locally built 87029 *Earl Marischal* waits departure from Platform 6 with a Manchester Piccadilly train. The majority of Manchester Inter-City trains ran via Stoke to avoid the speed restrictions imposed between Crewe and Sandbach, due to continued subsidence caused by salt extraction; these lakes created are known locally as 'flashes'.

24133 and 44008, Crewe North Junction, 21 January 1978

An unusual combination of 24133 and 44008 are bought together for the Class 44 farewell tour. About to take over from 44009, which had hauled the special from Nottingham via the Woodhead and Stockport, this pair then worked back to Nottingham via Chester, Shrewsbury, Walsall and Burton. Crewe provided the 24/1 for steam heat on what was a bitterly cold January day.

85007, Crewe North Junction, 23 October 1982

Usually diagrammed for Class 86 or 87 haulage, 85007 brings a Manchester Piccadilly to Euston service across North Junction in October 1982. These expresses were provided principally to serve Wilmslow, as the majority ran via the Potteries, leaving the Manchester line at Cheadle Hulme, therefore avoiding the permanent speed restrictions south of Sandbach.

85011, North Junction, June 1983

The 1 hour 20 minute 16.56 Euston–Manchester 'Manchester Pullman' was timed to set down only at Crewe at 18.49. 85011 pulls away after its one minute stop for Wilmslow and Manchester. The 'Liverpool Pullman' had also run through Crewe, but unlike the Manchester service, which was all Pullman, the Liverpool Pullman contained ordinary second-class coaches. Occasionally this stock was also used for WCML charter workings. Interestingly this Mk 2 stock was vacuum-only braked, so could not be hauled by Class 87 locomotives – the principle traction at the time.

Class 304s, Platform 3a and 4a, February 1973

Once an everyday sight, Class 304s allocated to Crewe electric and Longsight were used on stopping services to Liverpool Lime Street and Altrincham. Here two Class 304s wait on Platforms 4a and 3a for Altrincham and Lime Street, respectively. In the 1970s there was no stopping service south towards Stafford, or north beyond Weaver Junction, using EMUs.

08220, Crewe North Junction

08220 moves a departmental trip working from the Chester line, which consisted of scrap from Crewe Works and a department coach – possibly of LNWR origin. A long-term resident of Crewe Diesel Depot, 08220 was vacuum brake only.

31174, Crewe North Junction

Class 31 runs across the North Junction after arriving with the 12.30 Peterborough parcels, due at Crewe at 16.12. This working often produced a Class 31, which at the time was rare at Crewe. Very occasionally one would turn up on a Cardiff train, or ECS from Derby Litchurch Lane C&W Works.

46023, Crewe North Junction

In the same location as the Class 31, and another unusual sight (at least in the 1970s/early 1980s), a Class 46 'Peak', 46023, makes its way off the diesel depot onto the Chester line on an unknown working. With the closure of Derby Loco Works, 'Peaks' could be seen in Crewe Works again in 1983, when it undertook repairs on the remaining Class 45 locos. 46023 was transferred to the research department in December 1983, becoming 97402 (on paper), before eventually returning to Crewe to be broken up at Gresty Lane in March 1994.

40044, Crewe North Junction

40044 eases an empty tanker train from Rowley Regis to Stanlow & Thornton out of Down through No. 1 road, onto the Chester line. After Chester it will reverse at Hooton to gain the Ellesmere Port line. This diagram was timetabled via Basford Hall but on occasions it ran via the station.

86235, Crewe North Junction

86235 *Novelty* departs from Platform 1 on a northbound working with a mix of early and later Mk2 stock. This loco, along with 86214 *Sans Pareil*, carried the Rainhill Rocket 150 livery, applied for the 1979 celebrations. Both were named after locos in the original trial of 1829.

D1061, Crewe North Stabling Point, *c.* 1970

D1061 *Western Envoy* was built at Crewe in 1963 and, for a period in the early 1960s, both Western and Warship diesel hydraulics could be seen at Crewe on North & West services, via the Shrewsbury line. In the 1970s, a Western at Crewe was a very rare occurrence (apart from specials). I only remember seeing one: D1025 *Western Guardsman* on a Severn Tunnel Junction–Carlisle freight, around 1975. In the early 1970s the Shrewsbury line did see the occasional Hymek on Cardiff trains, and Warship on freights.

031, Crewe North Junction, February 1973

Class 304 EMU, 031, is seen departing Crewe for Liverpool Lime Street on a northbound slow working. Behind the EMU the old works and clock tower entrance can be seen; sadly this area was cleared in the mid-1970s. At the time some forward-thinking people could have seen this developed into the National Railway Museum – imagine the financial benefits that would have brought to the region.

031, Crewe North Junction, August 1980

Looking south towards the station, a Class 86 hauls the Down fast train, accelerating along the Liverpool line. Visible in the foreground is the long neck siding and, behind the loco, the Down Liverpool independents, still at a lower level as it climbs out of the tunnel under North Junction. The independents were notoriously hard to see. You could see them from the station car park, but even then you would be looking down on the roof of passing freight workings.

Crewe Coal Yard Signal Box

Crewe Coal Yard signal box is located by the Up slow line. At the north end of the former Thomas Street coal and goods yard is a London Midland & Scottish Railway type 13 design, which opened on 10 December 1939. It was fitted with a sixty-five-lever Railway Executive Committee frame, replacing a 1902-built London & North Western Railway type 4 design signal box, located 105 yards to the south on the opposite side of the line. Two individual function switches were commissioned on 6 September 1979, controlling emergency replacement of 116 signals in conjunction with the closure of Coppenhall Junction signal box. Levers 61 to 65 were removed some time prior to 1990, reducing the frame to sixty levers. (David Ingham)

Eagle Bridge, Crewe ETD, 17 September 1972

A Class 47 is caught about to cross the 'Eagle Bridge', which, from the mid-1970s, was the only access into the Works complex. This bridge had large cast eagles on each corner. Their origins have a mystery; apparently they were found in the Works foundry. The electric traction depot, which was holding an open day on this occasion, can be glimpsed underneath the bridge.

85035 and 85030, Crewe Electric Traction Depot, 2 June 1984

Three locally allocated Class 85s stand outside the ETD in June 1984. The depot had opened in 1960 with phase 1 of the WML electrification and, along with Longsight and Allerton, formed the original depots for the project. The depot was difficult for the public to see, being only glimpsed from the Chester line.

86030, Crewe Electric Traction Depot, 1982

Though this loco was allocated to Willesden, the LMR AC electric fleet could be found at any of the electric traction depots along the length of the WCML. Originally numbered E3105, 86030 was primarily a freight engine when seen here; it would later become 86430, being scrapped in 2005.

8176, Crewe Electric Traction Depot, 17 September 1972

Crewe Electric Traction Depot held an open day in in September 1972. Ex-Works Class 20 8176 was on display, along with more usual local classes of diesel and electric locos. In the background is the test coach (brake unit 1 ADM 45053) and a brake tender, used for the Crewe Works test train of the time.

Crewe Electric Traction Depot, 17 September 1972

Another view taken on the 1972 open day shows the Crewe steam breakdown crane demonstrating lifting a 16T mineral wagon. The area was between the 'Eagle Bridge' and Flag Lane Bridge, with the Works water tower just visible on the left and the BR print works in the background.

Crewe ETD, 17 September 1972

Our last view of the 1972 open day shows prototype Mk3 trailer first M11003, for use in the first HST set, and two Mk 2Ds. Derby built three Mk 3 trailer firsts for the Class 252 prototype HST set – this one is oddly prefixed M. The Midland Region would not require diesel HST sets until Western and Eastern Regions were completed. All three coaches had recently been completed at Derby C&W Works. The coaches stand on a short isolated section, electrified at 1,500 v DC, and used to test Class 76s, which were repaired at Crewe Works.

Crewe Steel Works Signal Box

Crewe Steel Works signal box is located by the Down main line at the western exit to Crewe Electric Traction Maintenance Depot, and is a London Midland & Scottish Railway type 11C design. It was fitted with a twenty-lever Railway Executive Committee frame that opened in 1935, replacing an earlier signal box, located 65 yards to the west, on the opposite side of the line. (David Ingram)

Beeston Castle & Tarporley Signal Box

Beeston Castle & Tarporley signal box is a London & North Western Railway type 5 design, fitted with a twenty-six-lever London & North Western Railway tappet frame that opened in 1915. It replaced an earlier signal box located a short distance to the north. By May 1988 the illuminated track diagram showed the signal box name as Beeston Castle, although it remains named Beeston Castle & Tarporley in the sectional appendix.

1784, Crewe Works, *c.* 1970

Over the years Crewe Works had responsibility for different classes – solely, or shared with other BREL locations. Crewe was the main works for Class 47s, and shared overhauls for Class 20s with Glasgow and Derby. Two Class 47s, including 1784, and an unidentified Class 20 stand in the test area alongside the traverser.

37138, Crewe Works Open Day, 6 June 1981

Class 37s were associated with Doncaster Works, though in the early 1980s Crewe started to undertake a refurbishment programme on the class. Awaiting entry into the workshops, 37138 is stabled on the de-fuelling point on an open day. It would leave the Works with the cab front cut straight above the buffers.

47428, Crewe Works Open Day, 20 September 1975

Same place, same event, different year. Gateshead-allocated 47428 also awaits entry to the workshops, though in 1975. On this occasion, amongst the numerous Class 40s, 47s, 50s and AC electrics, the Works contained a number of Class 27s and 76s.

81002, Crewe Works, 10 October 1983

81002 awaits attention in 1983. Built as E3003 in 1960, it was originally allocated to Crewe Electric Traction Depot. With the completion of WCML electrification the class was transferred to Glasgow Shields Road in 1975. Finishing its use restricted to ECS workings at Euston, 81002 was withdrawn in 1990 and is preserved as the oldest surviving AC electric loco.

86259, Crewe Works, 10 October 1983

Seen in the reception area, 86259 *Peter Pan*, formerly E3144/86045, was rebuilt with flexicoil sprung bogies, becoming a Class 86/2 in 1975. 86259 survives in full operational condition, in a version of early electric blue and named *Les Ross*.

50045, Crewe Works, *c.* 1976

Crewe overhauled the Class 50 fleet until the Works was transferred to Doncaster in 1977. Toward the end of the Works association with the Class, 50045 displays its number in the head code in the style the Western Region applied to its remaining Class 52 Western locos after head codes were discontinued. The Class 50s had been leased to BR initially, and years of hard work on Anglo-Scottish expresses was telling on the class, so they were transferred to the Western Region in poor condition. They therefore gained a poor reputation, which would only be addressed with the refurbishment programme undertaken at Doncaster.

20017, Crewe Works, January 1984

20017, built as early as 1957, was dismantled for component recovery between 1983 and 1984. Crewe had worked on Class 20s over the years, but shared the class with other BREL locations.

47574, Crewe Works, June 1984

47574's so-called 'silver' roof gives away its home depot of Stratford. The roof was actually BR coach grey, but was known as such as Stratford had painted its two silver Jubilee Class 47s with silver roofs. Previously 47174, it was renumbered 47574 in January 1981, when it was modified at Crewe with ETH fittings.

81013, Crewe Works, March 1983

81013 looks superb as it awaits release from the Works after an overhaul in 1983. The Works was always a fascinating place to visit – locomotives at every stage of the process could be seen. The sight of an ex-Works loco like this was impressive, if short-lived, as once in traffic the shine was soon lost.

56120, Crewe Works, March 1983

56120 was built at Crewe between June 1982 and competition in May 1983, when it was delivered to Tinsley. The class was built by Electroputere, Romania (56001–030), BREL Doncaster (56031–115) and then, to allow Doncaster to build Class 58s, construction for the final batch was moved to BREL Crewe, which built 56116–56135. In the 1970s obtaining stock from abroad was completely unknown. The nation's workshops built all rolling stock, supporting thousands of skilled jobs, even exporting stock. What a sad decline has been allowed by certain short-sighted governments intent on privatisation at any cost.

47379, Crewe Works, 6 June 1981

6 June 1981 was the occasion of the annual Works open day. On this day the Works contained twenty-seven Class 47s, amongst them was Immingham's 47379. At this time, it was one of two Class 47s fitted with experimental Multiple Unit (MU) wiring; the other was 47370. They were known to enthusiasts as 'Pinky' and 'Perky'.

37158, Crewe Works, August 1983
Another loco fresh from overhaul, Bristol Bath Road Depot's 37158 stands in the test area, in what would be its last classified repair. Soon after Crewe would enter a phase of rebuilding thirty-one of the class into an ETH fitted 37/4 sub-class.

47711, Crewe Works
For the Glasgow–Edinburgh 'push-pull' upgrade of the late 1970s, from 1979 twelve Class 47s were converted at Crewe Works becoming new sub-class 47/7. Former 47498 became 47711 in November 1979, being named *Greyfriars Bobby* at Edinburgh Waverley in April 1981.

E6024, Crewe Works, June 1970

Not a location readily associated with Southern Region locos, Crewe undertook work on Classes 33 and 73 to ease the load for Eastleigh Works in the late 1960s/early 1970s. Crewe had converted ten Class 71s to electro-diesel Class 74s in 1967. Ex-Works E6024 stands in the test area before release to traffic. During this period, this was a unique location where it was possible to view a SR Class 73 alongside a Class 76 Woodhead Electric loco.

E6105, Crewe Works, 1969

Ten surplus Class 71s were moved to Crewe Works in 1966 to be re-built as type HB (Large EDs). Once rebuilt they were numbered E6101–10, and classified as 74. Here E6105 stands on the de-fuelling area. This loco had been released from Crewe Works to the Southern Region in 1968 – its early return must have been due to a technical issue. With electronics that were ahead of their time, the class never fulfilled their potential. This was coupled with a reduction of work, which would see the class withdrawn after only ten years' service. (RailOnline)

6881, Crewe Works, June 1970

Like the Class 20s, Class 37s could be found undergoing attention at Crewe, and also at other BREL establishments. Here long term Landore allocated 6881, stands in the test area, with the Traverser in the background. It was renumbered 37181 in 1974, staying on the Western Region until 1986 when it moved to Thornaby.

37084, Crewe Works

With some buffer damage visible, Eastern Region 37084 awaits Works attention in the mid-1980s. The loco has already had the buffer beam valance cutaway from a previous BREL visit. This loco would later become 37712 and see further use in Spain on high-speed rail construction works.

82005, 22 September 1979

Seen in the test area, 82005 awaits attention in September 1979. The loco had been inside the Works for several months, but would be repaired and return to WCML service until eventually being limited to ECS workings between Euston and Willesden. Withdrawal came in November 1987.

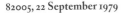

40084, Crewe Works, October 1983

A common sight within the Works complex, Crewe Works had been responsible for overhaul of the Class 40s since their introduction. No longer in service, 40084 had been withdrawn in May 1983 with a bogie fracture. It was cut up on-site in May 1984.

47521, 40064, 40168, Crewe Works, 24 September 1977

24 September 1977 saw the Works open day, a hugely popular event, as can be seen in this view taken in the erecting shop. Three type 4 locos are seen in various state of repair. 47521 would have been of interest as it was allocated to Holbeck and would not be seen in regular service locally. 40064 was one of a small batch of Scottish Class 40s, with fronts rebuilt from connecting doors to centre headcode. These were identifiable by the right-angle corners on the headcode box surround and the small protrusion on the lower edge where the doors had been.

**84008, Crewe Works,
August 1983**

Standing near the traverser
is long-term resident of the
Works, 84008, which was
withdrawn in October 1979,
though it would not be cut up
until November 1988.

**08222, Crewe Works,
September 1979**

Crewe Works had a
requirement for two or three
shunters to move stock
within the site. In the 1970s
Crewe Diesel Depot supplied
vacuum-braked Class 08s.
08222 had arrived at Crewe in
1959 as 13292 and remained
until withdrawal in 1984.

47105, Crewe Works, *c.* 1980

Cardiff Canton's 47105 awaits
entry to the diesel and electric
locomotive repair shop, also
known as the erecting shop,
in early 1980. It was possible
to eventually see BR's entire
fleet of Class 47s pass through
the Works – locos from
depots such as Thornaby or
Immingham were always a
good cop for local enthusiasts.

Crewe Works Electric Locomotive Repair Shop

Though they could be found in the erecting shop, electric locos had their own repair shop. A Class 87 and 85 receive attention in the electric locomotive repair shop (also known as the new repair shop), in the 1980s.

85040, Crewe Works, 6 February 1983

Devoid of its bogies, 85040 undergoes an overhaul in the erecting shop. Of the earlier AC electric classes, major work continued on Class 81 and 85 into the 1980s.

47299, Crewe Works, January 1984

47299 has an intriguing story. Built as D1866, it was renumbered under TOPS 47216 until 1981, when British Rail renumbered it after being contacted by a psychic who described in detail the loco's involvement in an accident. Sadly, even after changing identity, in December 1983 it was involved in a collision at Wrawby Junction. Whilst working the 15.02 Drax–Lindsay 900 ton empty oil tanks, it collided with the 17.32 Cleethorpes–Sheffield DMU. The crash remained noticeable after the repair as the new cabs were 2 inches higher than the rest of the bodyside lower profile, and the buffer beam lacked a raised edge. The two enthusiasts in this picture chat to the older gent, a retired railwayman, who would conduct tours on a Sunday afternoon, which you could join for a charity donation of 20p.

56131, Crewe Works, April 1984

Newly constructed 56131 stands in the paint shop, partway through receiving its large logo livery. Crewe would build another four Class 56, thus completing its order for the last nineteen locos of the class. The paint shop was one of the highlights of a Works visit, seeing new or overhauled locos in the final stage of completion.

47053, Crewe Works, 20 March 1984

This view of ex-Works 47053 shows the loco on the steep bank up to the 'Eagle Bridge' – at the time the only rail access to the Works complex. The bridge was visible outside the Works from the Victoria Avenue side, though you would be lucky to ever glimpse a loco using it.

81001, 84008, 81015, Flag Lane, Crewe Works, 15 June 1986

The area around the Flag Lane signal cabin was used for locos awaiting cutting up. This line includes 81001, 84008 and 81015. 81001 had caught fire hauling the 11.15 Euston–Stirling Motorail near Carstairs on 26 August 1983. 84008 had been withdrawn for seven years at this point, with 81015 withdrawn in December 1984, also after a fire.

82007, 83002, Crewe Works, 1977

82007 stands in the reception area as it awaits entry into the workshops. Suffering damage to the buffer beam and probably the frame, the cab had split from the body. 82007 was repaired and returned to service, lasting until eventual withdrawal in July 1983.

87032, Crewe Works, *c.* 1984

87032 *Kenilworth* near completion inside the erecting shop in the mid-1980s. Just beyond the loco was an internal traverser, above which stands the 50 ton overhead crane, which ran the length of the majority of the shop on the huge blue girders above the loco.

56133, Crewe Works, 4 June 1984

Specially prepared for the occasion, newly built 56133 was named *Crewe Locomotive Works* on the occasion of the Works open day on 4 June 1984. Soon after, 56133 would start work at Gateshead depot.

86247 *Abraham Darby*, Basford Hall Junction

86247 *Abraham Darby* approaches Basford Hall Junction with a northbound Inter-City express. The train contains the usual mix of air-conditioned Mk 2 and 3 stock, though is slightly longer than usual WCML Class 1 diagrams. Around 1980 one could sit at the lineside here and watch a continuous procession of BR blue-liveried locos passing with a variety of workings. Happy times indeed.